SHEEP

Flora Gandolfo

Grolier
an imprint of
◪SCHOLASTIC
www.scholastic.com/librarypublishing

Published 2009 by Grolier
An Imprint of Scholastic Library Publishing
Old Sherman Turnpike
Danbury, Connecticut 06816

For The Brown Reference Group plc
Project Editor: Jolyon Goddard
Picture Researchers: Clare Newman, Sophie
Mortimer
Designer: Sarah Williams
Managing Editor: Tim Harris

Volume ISBN-13: 978-0-7172-8054-4
Volume ISBN-10: 0-7172-8054-3

**Library of Congress
Cataloging-in-Publication Data**

Nature's children. Set 5.
    p. cm.
    Includes index.
    ISBN-13: 978-0-7172-8084-1
    ISBN-10: 0-7172-8084-5 (set)
    1. Animals--Encyclopedias, Juvenile. I.
Grolier (Firm)
    QL49.N386 2009
    590.3--dc22
                        2008014674

Printed and bound in China

PICTURE CREDITS

Front Cover: **Shutterstock**: Uschi Hering.

Back Cover: **Shutterstock**: Eric Gevaert,
Esther Groen, Joyfull, Bruce Parrott.

Ardea: Nick Gordon 46; **FLPA**: Peter Dean
34, Wayne Hutchinson 14, 41, Inga Spence 18,
Ariadne Van Zandbergen 33, Klaus-Peter Wolf
13; **Shutterstock**: Al Parker Photography
22, Henk Bentlage 5, Vera Bogaerts 38, Ken
Canning 37, Matthew Collingwood 2–3, Eric
Gevaert 26–27, Alexander Gitlits 30, Eric
Isselee 4, Adrian T. Jones 21, Anne Kitzman
45, Alex Melnick 29, nhtg 9, Suzan Oschmann
10, Bruce Parrott 6, Sandra Peek 42, Lee
Torrens 17.

Contents

FACT FILE: Sheep

Class	Mammals (Mammalia)
Order	Even-toed mammals (Artiodactyla)
Family	Cattle, antelope, sheep, and goats (Bovidae)
Genus	Sheep, including bighorn sheep, snow sheep, and domestic sheep (*Ovis*)
Species	Domestic sheep (*Ovis aries*)
World distribution	Domestic sheep are farmed worldwide; wild sheep still live in North America, Europe, North Africa, and Asia
Habitat	Farmland, hills, and mountains
Distinctive physical characteristics	Most have a woolly coat that varies in color from white to black; cloven hooves; males and some females have horns; the males' horns can be big and spiraling
Habits	Live in flocks; graze during the day; rams head butt one another during the breeding season
Diet	Grass and other meadow plants

Introduction

Farm, or **domestic**, sheep first came from the mountains of Asia. Like many other farm animals, domestic sheep spread with people as they moved around the world. Sheep are now a common sight in the fields and plains of Africa, Europe, Australia, New Zealand, and North and South America.

Sheep provide humans with meat, milk for cheese, **wool** for clothing and other fabrics, and many other products. Except for maybe cattle, no other animal is as useful to humans as sheep.

There are more than one billion domestic sheep in the world.

Sheep usually live to about 12 years, although some have reached 20 years.

Sheep Basics

A sheep's woolly coat is called a **fleece**. The fleece can be black, brown, gray, or white. Sometimes it is a mixture of these colors.

Some kinds, or **breeds**, of sheep have horns that curl in a spiral on the sides of their head. Some breeds have three or even four horns and others, known as **polled** sheep, have no horns at all.

Ewes, or female sheep, can weigh between 100 and 225 pounds (45 to 100 kg). Male sheep, or **rams**, are usually larger and weigh between 100 and 350 pounds (45 to 160 kg).

Like humans, adult sheep have 32 teeth. However, their front teeth, or **incisors**, grow only from the lower jaw. Incisors are sharp teeth that cut food. When sheep chomp grass, the incisors press against a hard, toothless pad on the upper surface of the mouth.

Sticking Together

A group of sheep is called a **flock**. Sheep naturally like to be in a group, and that helps make them easy to farm. A farmer can move sheep around easily, since they tend to follow one another around.

Sheep can also survive harsh weather, which makes them popular with farmers. Sheep can live happily in hot, dry desert climates or in cold, rainy, hilly places. Sheep eat almost any type of grass, herb, or shrub, although they usually graze only on low-growing plants.

Their hard, hornlike **hooves** are split down the middle. These types of hooves are called **cloven**. Other types of animals that have cloven hooves include cattle and goats.

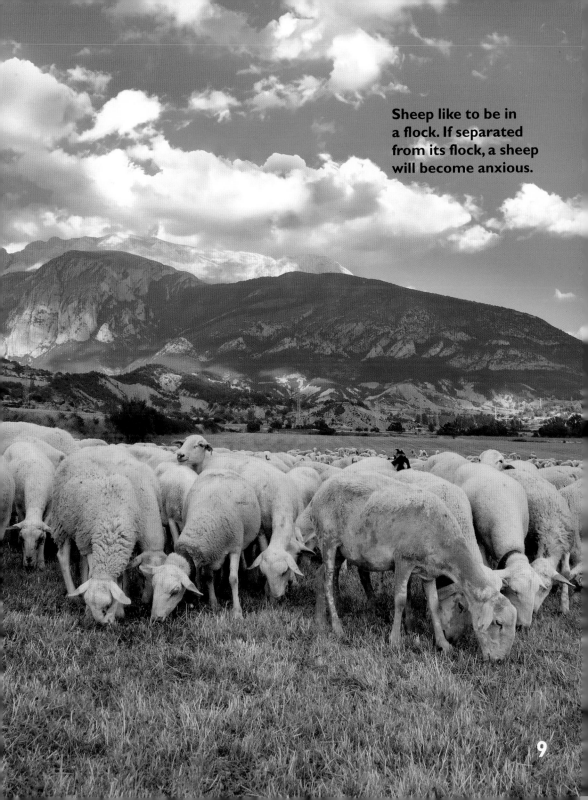

Sheep like to be in a flock. If separated from its flock, a sheep will become anxious.

Many animals chew the cud, including sheep, goats, cattle, deer, giraffes, bison, and camels.

Chomp and Chew

Sheep are plant eaters, or **herbivores**. They live entirely on grass and other plants that do not grow very tall. Sheep spend a lot of time grazing. They also spend a lot of time chewing. Their stomach has four parts, or chambers, unlike a human stomach, which is just one chamber. When sheep swallow their grassy food, it is stored in the first stomach chamber, where it is broken down into a soft paste called **cud**. Later in the day, the cud moves back up into the mouth, and the sheep gives it a second chew. This process is called chewing the cud, or **ruminating**. When the cud is swallowed again, it passes through the other stomach chambers and the rest of the **digestive system**.

Chewing the cud helps sheep get as many **nutrients** as possible from their food. It also allows them to eat large amounts of grass quickly. They can then chew it slowly later, while keeping an eye out for danger.

Sheep in History

Sheep are one of humankind's oldest friends. They have provided us with food and clothing for thousands of years. Ancient people tamed them from the wild and raised them as farm animals more than 10,000 years ago. Many civilizations have been built on sheep farming. In fact, in some parts of the world even today a person's wealth is measured by how many sheep he or she owns.

Scientists think that modern sheep are the **descendants** of two types of wild sheep called the mouflon (MOO-FLON) and the urial (URR-EE-UL). These sheep still live in the wilds of southeastern Europe and Asia. The first domestic sheep did not have a thick woolly fleece like the sheep of today. They had a hairy coat like a goat or cow. By choosing which sheep could **mate**, humans have over the centuries created today's woolly varieties of sheep.

Now rare in its natural habitat, the mouflon is the smallest type of wild sheep. It stands 28 inches (70 cm) at the shoulders.

13

The Cheviot first came from the Cheviot Hills, where England and Scotland meet. This breed is raised for both its wool and meat.

Many Breeds

There are more than a thousand breeds of sheep in the world. More than 40 breeds are farmed in the United States alone. In fact, there are more breeds of sheep than any other livestock species! They can be very different from one another. Some, such as the Cheviot, have a white face. Others, such as the Hampshire or Oxford, have a dark brown or even black face.

Different breeds are raised for different uses. Some are raised for meat, some for their milk, and others for their wool. Sheep bred for wool have a thick fleecy coat, whereas those bred for meat are fleshy and fat. There are still some breeds of sheep today that, like their wild **ancestors**, are not woolly at all. These breeds are called hair sheep. They are usually raised for their hide and meat.

Merino Sheep

Christopher Columbus brought the first domestic sheep to the Americas in 1493. About that time, the Spanish were one of the greatest producers of sheep in Europe. Their best breed was the fine-wooled merino. Merino wool dominated the wool trade and brought the Spanish great wealth. That helped Spain pay for the voyages of the early Spanish conquerors of the Americas.

Merino sheep are still prized for their fine wool. Many of today's newer breeds have distant relatives in the merino family.

Merinos are fairly small and have a white face and whitish fleece. Their wool is soft and heavy. An adult merino ewe can produce 10 pounds (4.5 kg) of wool each year, and a ram can give 20 pounds (9 kg) of wool. The wool can be sold at market for a very good price. A flock of merinos is extremely valuable!

Merinos are the
best known of
all wool sheep.

17

This ewe and her lambs live on a sheep farm in Nevada.

18

Today's Sheep

The countries in the world that raise the most sheep today are China, Australia, New Zealand, Argentina, the United States, and the United Kingdom.

In North America, sheep farming is a big industry. Sheep are raised mainly for their meat. Most sheep are located to the west of the Mississippi River. The sheep range in vast unfenced areas and live in flocks of as many as 2,000 animals. Small sheep farms have flocks of about 200 sheep. The farmer moves the flocks from one place to the next in search of the best grassland, or pasture. The biggest sheep-raising state is Texas, with California, South Dakota, and Colorado close behind.

Family Ties

Breeding is very important for raising sheep. It keeps the flock a healthy size. Farmers choose the best animals to breed. These sheep then pass on their good features and improve the overall quality of the flock. Rams can be chosen from their own flock. They can also be bought from a sheep market for their qualities that the farmer wants to pass on to his flock.

Most ewes breed and give birth once a year. All the ewes in a flock are usually ready to breed at the same time of year. That is called being in season, or ready to mate. Ewes are in season any time between August and September, depending on the breed and where the sheep live. When a ewe is ready to mate, she releases a scent. The ram picks up the scent and knows that she is ready.

The bigger a ram's horns, the more likely he is to win fights with other rams and impress the ewes.

A pair of bighorn rams head butt each other. Bighorn sheep are wild relatives of domestic sheep. They live in North America.

Rutting and Butting

In the wild, rams fight when ewes are in season. They show off their strength to scare other rams away and attract females. They charge at one another and crash their heads together, tangling their horns. The fighting is called **rutting**, and the horn clashing is called butting.

The rutting season can go on for several months. Rutting rams can cause serious injuries and can even kill one another! During this time they are very **aggressive** and may even butt the farmer. The rams, therefore, need very careful handling.

In domestic flocks, the farmer carefully separates the ewes into groups of about 30 animals. One ram is let loose within each group, and he mates with all the ewes. The ewes soon become pregnant.

Mother Ewes

A ewe's pregnancy lasts about five months. Farmers give pregnant ewes special attention to make sure they have shelter, extra food and water, and plenty of exercise during their pregnancy. The extra attention helps them produce healthy **lambs**.

When a ewe becomes restless and starts to look for a private place or shelter, the farmer knows it is time for her to give birth. The farmer may call a vet to help with the birth. The vet might massage the ewe's belly and make sure the lamb is in the right position to come out.

Many breeds of sheep give birth in spring, and this time is known as the lambing season. The birth usually takes one to three hours and produces a single lamb or twins.

Leaping Lambs

After the birth, the ewe licks her lamb clean. It can get onto its feet very quickly, about an hour after it is born! The lamb is soon **nursing**, or drinking its mother's milk. If there are nursing problems, the farmer might feed the lamb with a bottle.

Sometimes farmers keep the tiny newborn lambs in small pens with their mothers. That way, they can watch the lambs' progress and make sure there are no problems.

Like all young mammals, lambs are very playful. They chase one another and leap around. But they never stray too far from their mothers.

By about three weeks old, lambs are taking their first mouthfuls of grass, as well as still drinking their mother's milk. This process of gradually moving on to an adult diet is called **weaning.** The young sheep are usually fully weaned by four or five months.

Farmers tag their lambs'
ears to help them identify
their sheep.

Woolly Sheep

For thousands of years, people have depended on sheep's wool to make warm, long-lasting material for clothing, blankets, felt, and other fabrics.

Sheep's fleeces are shaved off in a process called **shearing**. The wool is then cleaned, bleached or dyed, and spun into yarn. Yarn is used to make fabrics or knitted into sweaters.

Breeds of sheep that are raised for their wool can be divided into fine wool breeds, long wool breeds, and coarse wool breeds. The wool from fine wool breeds, such as merinos and Rambouillets (RAM-BUH-LAYZ), is usually made into clothing. Other types of wool have different uses. For example, coarse wool—from breeds such as the Romney—is often used to make rugs and carpets.

Individual wool
fibers appear
scaly under a
microscope. The
fibers also have
many kinks, or
crimps, which
make the fibers
soft and fuzzy.

29

If held in a comfortable position, a sheep will not struggle during shearing.

Sheepshearing

Sheep farmers, or **shepherds**, shear their flocks
once a year, usually in the late spring when the
weather is getting warm. Then the sheep will
not miss their heavy coat! In some countries,
shearing is still done by hand with a pair of
large scissors called shears.

Electric shears are much quicker. Professional
sheepshearers often go from place to place
shearing whole flocks. An expert shearer takes
only a few minutes to shear each animal. They
shear off the coat in one neat piece. Good
shearers pride themselves on their speed and
efficiency. In some countries, they even hold
sheepshearing competitions to find out who
is the quickest!

Measuring Wool

One sheep produces between 2 to 30 pounds (1 to 14 kg) of wool each year. When the fleece has been taken off the sheep, it is rolled, tied, and sent to market. There, it is washed and valued depending on its weight and quality.

There are several ways of valuing wool. The spinning count is the oldest method. It is based on how many yards of yarn are produced by 1 pound (0.45 kg) of clean wool. The blood system was originally based on how many of the sheep's ancestors were merino. Nobody today really keeps track of how much merino blood is in the flock, but the system is still used sometimes to describe the quality of a breed's wool. The micron system is the most modern and scientific system. It is very accurate because people measure the width, or diameter, of the wool fiber. Fine wool sheep have fibers with a diameter up to 20 microns. (One micron, or micrometer, equals one-millionth of a meter.)

A Berber woman from Tunisia, in North Africa, spins wool into yarn.

35

A farmer milks her
flock of ewes in a m

Other Products

After wool, meat is the second most common product from sheep. Meat from young sheep is called lamb, and meat from adult sheep is called **mutton**. Some sheep are also raised for their milk. It is used to make many types of cheese, including French Roquefort.

The hides, or skins, of sheep are used to make chammy (SHA-MEE), a soft cloth that is often used to polish cars. The hides from hair sheep make the best type of leather, which is much tougher than the leather from other sheep breeds.

Lanolin is a waxy substance that is made by the sheep's skin. It keeps the fleece waterproof. It is extracted from raw wool and is a key ingredient in many cosmetics and beauty aids, such as lipsticks, shampoos, conditioners, and lotions. Lanolin is also used in shoe polish, glue, soap, car oil, printing ink, and fertilizer. Tallow, or fat from sheep, was once commonly used to make candles and soap. The guts of sheep were also used to make the strings of musical instruments.

Wild Cousins

Most sheep in the world today are domestic sheep, living under the care of humans. However, there are still many types of wild sheep living in Asia, North Africa, Europe, and North America. Some of these are domestic sheep that have gone back to a wild existence. Domestic animals that return to live wild are called **feral**. Other types of wild sheep are different species from domestic sheep. They include blue sheep, Barbary sheep, bighorn sheep, thinhorn sheep, urials, argalis (AR-GUH-LEEZ), mouflons, and snow sheep. These sheep do not have the woolly fleece of their domestic relatives. In fact, many of them have short hair and look more like goats than sheep.

Their habits are very similar, and they move around in herds looking for pasture to graze. Their herds differ from domestic flocks in that they are smaller, usually with fewer than 50 sheep. The rams tend to live apart from the flock, alone or with other rams. They only join the flock during the breeding season.

A bighorn ewe searches in the snow for grass to eat. Bighorns have never been domesticated.

Traditional shepherds
tend their flock in
northern India.

Shepherds

Traditional shepherds still farm sheep in many countries around the world, including the United States. Shepherds spend their life moving their flock from place to place looking for pasture. They sometimes move upward into mountains to find good grazing. They might stay there for as long as six months, often with only the company of their flock.

Shepherds feed extra hay to their flock in winter when it is harder to find grass to graze. They also make sure the sheep have a constant supply of freshwater. However, shepherds are now rare in many countries, as more and more modern, large-scale sheep farms take over from traditional ways of farming.

Sheepdogs

For thousands of years, sheepdogs have been helping shepherds in their work. Also called herding dogs, these clever and courageous animals are loyal to their flock and their human master. They sometimes even risk their life to protect the sheep against wild animals, such as bears, big cats, and wolves, and other dangers. Sheep become stressed when they are separated from their flock, and a sheepdog will make sure that any lost sheep are brought back to the group. They also guard the flock at night when the shepherd and sheep are asleep and raise the alarm in case of danger.

It takes a lot of skill to manage a sheepdog. The dog and the shepherd have a close bond. The shepherd often controls and communicates with the dog by using whistles, calls, and hand signals. Under the watchful eye of the shepherd, the dog can keep a large flock of sheep together.

Border collies are excellent at rounding up sheep.

This ewe is bleating because she cannot find her lamb.

Sheep Senses

Sheep are shy creatures that get frightened easily. In nature, they are a **prey** animal, which means that meat eaters, such as wolves and big cats, hunt them. For that reason, they are always wary of danger.

Their eyes, placed on the sides of their head, give sheep a wide field of vision—they can see behind them without turning their head! That allows them to spot **predators** early. They also have an excellent sense of smell, which helps warn them of approaching danger.

What sound do sheep make? The "baa baa" **bleat** is only part of the answer. Ewes and lambs bleat. Rams, however, are almost completely silent. The only sound they make is a hissing sound through their nostrils when they chase ewes during the breeding season.

Ewes also make a barking sound, but that is rare. They make this sound only when they become worried or frightened, such as when they see, hear, or smell a predator.

Goats and Sheep

Sheep are distantly related to goats, and they share many similar features. In fact, some breeds of sheep and goats are so similar that it can be difficult to tell which is which! The easiest way to tell them apart is by looking at the tail. A goat's tail usually points upward, whereas a sheep's tail hangs down. Farmers often snip the end off the sheep's tail because it is easier to keep the animal clean and healthy. This cut is called docking.

Goats and sheep also eat different kinds of plants. Sheep graze on grass and other low-growing plants. Goats eat grass, too, but also like to eat twigs from taller plants such as shrubs. Some goats will even climb trees to eat shoots and branches. Eating the shoots of shrubs and trees is called browsing.

Unlike a sheep, a goat's
tail points upward.

45

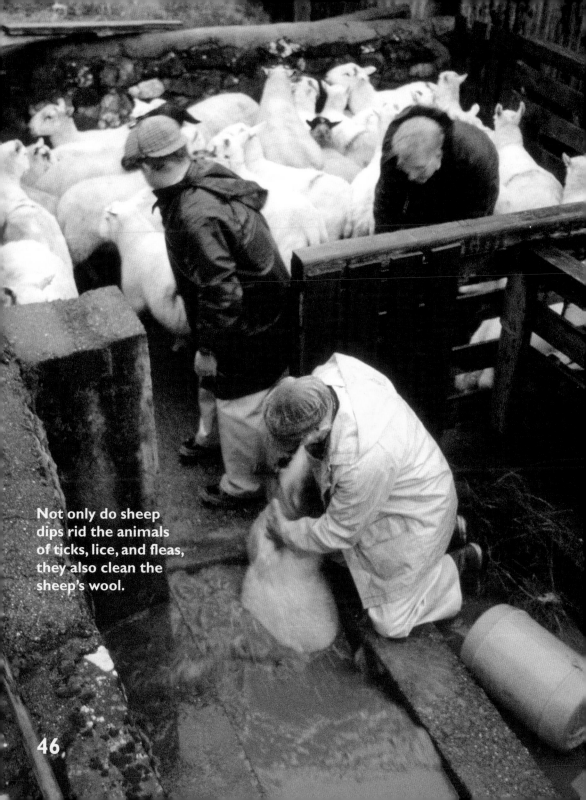

Not only do sheep dips rid the animals of ticks, lice, and fleas, they also clean the sheep's wool.

Sick Sheep

Like all domestic animals, sheep need protection from diseases and pests. Ticks, lice, and fleas are all small pests that can make sheep very uncomfortable and nervous. These pests can attach themselves to the fleece and skin and feed off the animal's blood. They can damage whole flocks if sheep are not treated for them. One way to get rid of these pests is to dip the sheep in a solution that kills the pests.

Sheep can also suffer from worms that live in their intestines. Many sheep diseases can be cured with medicines. Others, such as bluetongue and foot-and-mouth disease, are much more serious. Whole flocks of sheep might have to be slaughtered to stop the spread of these diseases.

Other Dangers

Sheep are nervous animals. Even pet dogs can make them frightened. That can be very bad for their health. Stress and anxiety can sometimes cause sheep to collapse. Predators, such as coyotes, wolves, and cougars, are a threat to flocks. A ram might defend itself against attack, charging with its horns lowered, but ewes and lambs are more likely to run.

Sheepdogs are not the only animals that have been used to protect sheep. Farmers have also used donkeys, cows, and even llamas to guard sheep. These animals are big enough to chase or scare away predators. Farmers and shepherds certainly have to work hard to make sure their flocks can graze, chew the cud, and sleep in predator-free peace!

Words to Know

Aggressive	Angry and ready to fight.
Ancestors	Early types of a particular animal.
Bleat	The "baa baa" sound made by a lamb or ewe.
Breeding	Producing young or babies.
Breeds	Kinds of sheep, each with its own characteristics.
Cloven	Type of hoof that is split into two.
Cud	Swallowed food that is brought back into the mouth for chewing a second time. Cud is a paste.
Descendants	The offspring, their offspring, and so on of an animal.
Digestive system	The parts of an animal's body, such as the stomach and intestines, that extract nutrients from food.
Domestic	Raised by humans.
Ewes	Adult female sheep.
Feral	Domestic animals that have returned to the wild.
Fleece	The woolly coat of a sheep.
Flock	A herd or group of sheep.
Herbivores	Animals that eat plants.

49

Hooves	Giant, thickened nails surrounding the feet of sheep.
Incisors	The sharp front teeth that are used for cutting food.
Lambs	Young sheep.
Mate	To come together to produce young.
Mutton	Meat of an adult sheep.
Nursing	Drinking the mother's milk.
Nutrients	The components of foods—such as proteins, fats, sugars—needed by animals to live and grow.
Polled	Without horns.
Predators	Animals that hunt other animals.
Prey	An animal hunted by other animals.
Rams	Adult male sheep.
Ruminating	Double-chewing food. Another term for chewing the cud.
Rutting	Fighting between rams during the breeding season.
Shearing	Shaving off a sheep's fleece.
Shepherds	Farmers who look after sheep.
Weaning	Replacing milk with the food an adult animal eats.
Wool	The fuzzy hair of sheep.

Find Out More

Books

Jackson, T. *Bighorn Sheep*. Nature's Children. Danbury, Connecticut: Grolier, 2008.

Miller, S. S. *Sheep*. True Books. Danbury, Connecticut: Children's Press, 2000.

Web sites

All About Sheep for Kids
www.kiddyhouse.com/Farm/Sheep/
Tons of information about sheep.

Sheep
www.enchantedlearning.com/subjects/mammals/farm/Sheepprintout.shtml
Facts about sheep and a printout to color in.

Index